CLIMATE CHANGE

KATIE DICKER

Published in 2025 by Cavendish Square Publishing, LLC
2544 Clinton Street, Buffalo, NY 14224

First published in Great Britain in 2024 by Hodder & Stoughton
Copyright © Hodder & Stoughton, 2024

No part of this publication may be reproduced, stored in a retrieval system, or transmitted in any form or by any means—electronic, mechanical, photocopying, recording, or otherwise—without the prior permission of the copyright owner. Request for permission should be addressed to Permissions, Cavendish Square Publishing, 2544 Clinton Street, Buffalo, NY 14224. Tel (877) 980-4450; fax (877) 980-4454.

Website: cavendishsq.com

This publication represents the opinions and views of the author based on his or her personal experience, knowledge, and research. The information in this book serves as a general guide only. The author and publisher have used their best efforts in preparing this book and disclaim liability rising directly or indirectly from the use and application of this book.

The website addresses (URLs) included in this book were valid at the time of going to press. However, it is possible that contents or addresses may have changed since the publication of this book. No responsibility for any such changes can be accepted by either the author or the publisher.

Editor: Katie Dicker
Designer: Clare Nicholas
Series Designer: Dan Prescott

Picture acknowledgements:
Shutterstock: EfteskiStudio cover t and 29, shuttermuse cover b, asadykov 4, Petr Klabal 5, SN040288 7, Arthur Villator 8, worldclassphoto 10, FloridaStock 12, evgenii mitroshin 13, fenkieandreas 14, Gema Alvarez Fernandez 15, Leonid Andronov 16-17, Diyana Dimitrova 17t, Magdanatka 18, Roman Mikhailiuk 19, Smile Fight 20, TonyV3112 21, Denis Zhitnik 22, David Buzzard 24, Westock Productions 26, Holli 28; Alamy: 506 collection 6, Xinhua 11, Klaus Ohlenschlaeger 23, Dinodia Photos 25, industryview 27; Getty: Antonio Busiello 9.

All design elements from Shutterstock.

Every attempt has been made to clear copyright. Should there be any inadvertent omission,
please apply to the publisher for rectification.

Cataloging-in-Publication Data

Names: Dicker, Katie.
Title: Climate change / Katie Dicker.
Description: Buffalo, NY : Cavendish Square Publishing, 2025. | Series: What can we do? | Includes glossary and index.
Identifiers: ISBN 9781502673763 (pbk.) | ISBN 9781502673770 (library bound) | ISBN 9781502673787 (ebook)
Subjects: LCSH: Climatic changes--Juvenile literature. | Environmental policy--Citizen participation--Juvenile literature.
Classification: LCC QC903.15 D53 2025 | DDC 551.6--dc23

CPSIA compliance information: Batch #CW25CSQ: For further information contact Cavendish Square Publishing LLC at 1-877-980-4450.

Printed in the United States of America

CONTENTS

What is climate change?	4
Taking action	6
Changing weather	8
The Amazon Rainforest	10
Melting ice	12
Ocean impact	14
Energy for buildings	16
The food we eat	18
The way we travel	20
Shopping habits	22
The power of tech	24
Reduce, repair, reuse, recycle	26
Speaking out	28
Glossary	30
Further information	31
Index	32

WHAT IS CLIMATE CHANGE?

Have you heard news stories about floods, intense heatwaves, or rising sea levels? These events are becoming more common because of climate change – a long-term shift in our planet's temperatures and weather patterns. Although natural conditions have triggered gradual climate change in the past, human activity is causing our environment to change at a faster rate.

When power plants and factories burn fossil fuels, they release gases such as carbon dioxide and methane into the atmosphere.

Greenhouse gases

Before the Industrial Revolution (1750–1900), the average global annual temperature on Earth was about 56.7°F (13.7°C). Natural gases in the atmosphere, such as carbon dioxide (CO_2), absorbed the Sun's heat, forming a protective layer around Earth and keeping our planet at a suitable temperature for life. Then, as countries began to develop in the 18th century, they used fossil fuels such as coal, oil, and gas to run vehicles, heat buildings, and power factories. These fuels release more "greenhouse gases" when they're burnt, trapping more of the Sun's heat and causing temperatures to rise. These additional gases (known collectively as "carbon emissions") are causing our climate to change.

Lost vegetation

At the same time, forests have been cleared for building, for mining, and for agricultural land to feed our growing population. Trees and other plants absorb carbon dioxide, maintaining a healthy balance of gases in the atmosphere. When they're cut down, this balance is disrupted. If the cut-down trees are burnt or left to rot, their stored carbon is released back into the atmosphere, tipping the balance even further.

Where are we now?

Today, greenhouse gases in the atmosphere are at their highest level for two million years – over 400 parts per million – and rising. Since the late 1800s, average temperatures on Earth have risen. These warmer temperatures are challenging the delicate balance of our natural world and we're beginning to see the damage. This book looks at the causes and effects of climate change, how we can adapt to changing conditions and what we can all do to help reduce its impact.

IT'S A FACT

Since 1850, Earth's temperature has risen by an average of 0.11°F (0.06°C) every decade. But since 1981, this rate of warming has more than doubled per decade.

The Mauna Loa Observatory in Hawaii, USA – 11,145 feet (3,397 m) above sea level – has been collecting atmospheric data since the 1950s, which shows a sharp increase in CO_2 levels.

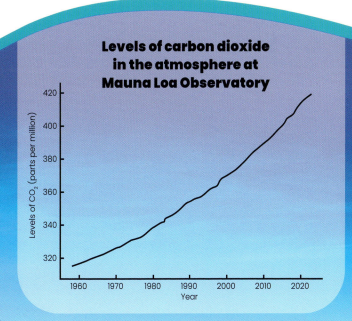

Levels of carbon dioxide in the atmosphere at Mauna Loa Observatory

TAKING ACTION

In the 1900s, some scientists began to suggest Earth's climate was warming and that increased levels of carbon dioxide were to blame. But other scientists thought it was impossible for human activity to affect such a huge system as Earth's climate. By the 1980s, however, the evidence was more compelling, and the scientific community began to unite and call for action.

International response

In 1988, the United Nations (UN) set up an international group to look at the scientific evidence and to advise governments on climate data. Then in 1992, over 150 nations agreed to work together to take action on climate change. As more nations joined in, they met at annual conferences to monitor the situation.

At the 21st meeting in Paris, in 2015, nearly every country in the world agreed to limit a rise in temperatures to well below 2°C, or 3.6°F, compared to pre-industrial levels, by imposing further cuts to their carbon emissions.

Then US Secretary of State, John Kerry, with his granddaughter, as he signs the Paris Agreement in 2015.

Net zero

Scientists now know we need to limit the temperature rise to 2.7°F (1.5°C) to maintain a healthy climate. To do this, we need to reach "net zero" by 2050. This means balancing the amount of carbon emissions produced with the amount removed from the atmosphere, so the climate remains stable. Since 2019, more than 120 countries have committed to a target of net zero by 2050. This requires governments and businesses to act fast, and for us all to change our behavior.

RACE TO ZERO

At a UN Climate Change Conference in 2019, a global campaign was launched to encourage companies, cities, regions, and other institutions to join the "Race to Zero" by promising to take immediate action to reduce carbon emissions. The clothing company, Levi Strauss, for example, pledged to get all its electricity from renewable sources (such as wind power or solar power) by 2025. It had already reached 85 percent of its target by 2021.

Levi Strauss has pledged to power all its factories and shops with renewable energy and to reduce carbon emissions in its supply chain too.

CHANGING WEATHER

Climate change isn't just about temperatures getting warmer. Our changing climate has an impact on weather patterns, too, putting plant and animal life at risk. Extreme weather events are also becoming more common, putting human lives in danger. But we can take action to protect our climate and to adapt to the conditions we're facing.

Warmer and wetter

Warmer temperatures mean drier conditions, so droughts are becoming more common and more intense. Wildfires are spreading more easily, and a shortage of water puts plants, animals, and food crops at risk. But warmer temperatures also cause more water evaporation, increasing the frequency and intensity of rainfall and bringing a risk of flooding, water pollution, and landslides. As sea temperatures warm (see page 12), tropical storms have increased in intensity and are traveling more slowly, putting lives, property, and infrastructure at risk.

The effects of climate change mean that tropical storms are now more likely to have wind speeds of more than 60 miles (100 km) per hour, battering coastlines and bringing storm surges and flooding.

Adapting to change

While we work to reduce carbon emissions, we also need to find ways to adapt to our changing climate. Scientists are developing climate-resistant crops that can withstand warmer, drier, or wetter conditions. The construction industry is building hurricane-proof structures and raising buildings in flood-prone areas, while water conservation projects provide back-up supplies in times of drought. Natural restoration projects in vulnerable areas – helping to restore forests, grasslands, wetlands, and coral reefs, for example – are also helping to reduce the impact of climate change.

NATURAL PROTECTION

In 1987, the state of Rajasthan, India, experienced a devastating drought that led to extreme shortages of drinking water and animal feed. Over 85 million people were severely affected. To avoid the crisis happening again, local communities began to regenerate forests in the region. The trees helped to raise groundwater levels by several feet and improved soil fertility, making communities more resilient to drier conditions.

A mangrove restoration project in Honduras is helping to reduce coastal erosion from stronger wind and waves. Mangroves can also store four times more carbon than mature tropical trees.

THE AMAZON RAINFOREST

The Amazon Rainforest is the largest rainforest in the world, spanning twice the size of India. It absorbs a quarter of all the carbon dioxide taken in by forests worldwide and plays a crucial role in transferring water from the ground to the atmosphere. But parts of the rainforest are being cut down at an alarming rate – for agriculture, building, and mining – putting our climate at risk.

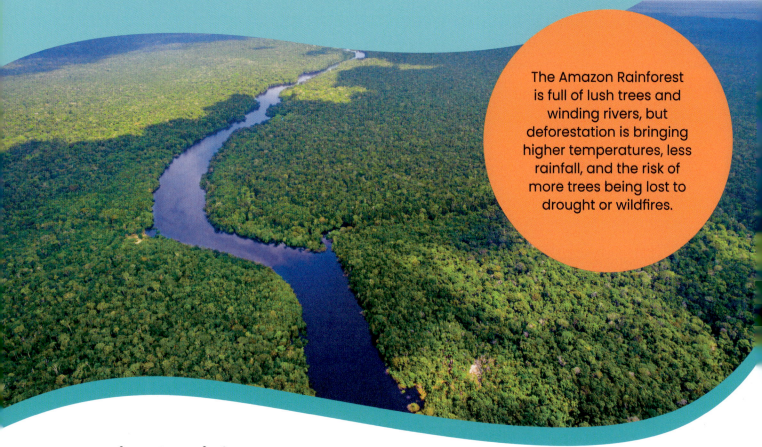

The Amazon Rainforest is full of lush trees and winding rivers, but deforestation is bringing higher temperatures, less rainfall, and the risk of more trees being lost to drought or wildfires.

Protecting the rainforest

Most of the Amazon's deforestation is linked to farming – to clear land for cattle, for palm oil plantations, and for soya farms (to grow animal feed). The rainforest spans eight South American countries but is mostly found in Brazil. Deforestation in the region has been difficult to regulate, but international pressure and fines have brought some protection. With scientific data showing the devastating impact of tree-loss on our climate, over 140 countries agreed to end deforestation by 2030 at a UN Climate Change Conference in 2021.

What Can I Do?

The Amazon Rainforest may be far away, but there are many things you can do to protect it:

- Avoid food choices that might impact the Amazon, such as Amazonian beef, and soybean products.

- Use less paper and wood – use recycled or "tree-free" paper, reuse scrap paper, and avoid paper plates and cups.

- Look for wood and paper products endorsed by the Forest Stewardship Council (FSC), which supports sustainable forest management, and palm oil products endorsed by the Roundtable on Sustainable Palm Oil (RSPO).

A trillion trees

There used to be about six trillion trees on Earth, but *half* of these have been cut down for development. Studies have shown that it's possible for us to restore up to one trillion trees without encroaching on agricultural land. In 2020, the World Economic Forum launched a global initiative to conserve, restore, and grow one trillion trees by 2030. Pakistan has committed to planting 10 billion trees and Colombia to 180 million, for example. Businesses, charities, cities, and states have also pledged their support.

China's president Xi Jinping joins a tree-planting initiative in Beijing. As part of the trillion trees project, China intends to plant and conserve 70 billion trees by 2030.

IT'S A FACT

An additional one trillion trees, once fully grown, could capture over a sixth of our carbon emissions. Regenerating forests can also improve local water quality and reduce soil erosion.

MELTING ICE

Rising temperatures are causing ice to melt in Earth's polar regions, disrupting the natural balance of our planet. When white snow and ice is lost, less heat from the Sun is reflected back into space. When frozen ground thaws, stored methane – a powerful greenhouse gas – can be released into the atmosphere. We need to keep temperature rises to a minimum while we adapt to these changing conditions.

Far-reaching effects

When polar ice melts, the ocean water warms below, which means the polar regions are warming three times as fast as the rest of the planet. These temperature changes are affecting weather patterns and animals are having to adapt. Freeze-thaw cycles are becoming more common, for example. When rain falls on soft snow and freezes, it forms a hard ice layer preventing herbivores, such as reindeer, from reaching their plant food. As sea levels rise (see page 14), coastal communities around the world are also at risk.

Polar bears rely on the Arctic sea ice to hunt seals, but the summer ice has shrunk by about 13 percent per decade in recent years.

Working together

The melting ice has also brought opportunities for economic development in the region – with new shipping routes available, and increased access to oil, gas, rare metals, and fish stocks. Rules and regulations try to ensure this development is sustainable, and conservation projects protect the most vulnerable regions. Scientists are also working with Indigenous communities to work out the best ways to manage the changing climate conditions.

THE ARCTIC COUNCIL

In 1996, the Arctic Council was set up to encourage cooperation in environmental protection in the region. Its eight Arctic member states (Canada, Denmark, Finland, Iceland, Norway, Sweden, Russia, and the United States) have been joined by Indigenous groups and observing countries and organizations who share their expertise. Arctic Council projects and initiatives bring Arctic issues to worldwide attention and advise the international community on policy recommendations. Meanwhile, scientists are also looking at ways to help protect and restore the Arctic ice (see page 25).

The Arctic is home to about 4 million people who have rich knowledge about the region and its weather patterns.

OCEAN IMPACT

Our oceans absorb heat and carbon dioxide from our atmosphere, helping to keep our climate stable. But with increased carbon emissions, our oceans are absorbing more heat and carbon than ever before. As the water becomes more acidic, marine life is endangered, and rising sea levels are putting low-lying settlements at risk. Ocean conservation has become a pressing issue.

Changing conditions

Our oceans absorb about 90 percent of excess heat in the atmosphere and around 30 percent of our carbon emissions. When ocean water becomes more acidic, some organisms are unable to form the shells they need to survive, while less oxygen endangers marine life and coral reefs.

Sea levels are rising partly because warm water expands and partly because melting glaciers are adding to its volume, putting low-lying coastal communities and islands at risk of flooding and shoreline disintegration. Ocean currents and weather patterns are also being disrupted.

A scuba diver in Indonesia observes coral bleaching, caused by unusually warm sea temperatures over an extended period of time.

Protecting the seas

While we work to reduce carbon emissions and remove carbon from our atmosphere (see page 24), conservation projects work to preserve ocean life. Over 70 countries in the Global Ocean Alliance are working to protect at least 30 percent of our oceans by 2030, with targeted projects and marine protection areas. Coral reefs are being restored and breeding programs are helping marine life to adapt to warmer waters. Regulations have also tightened on fishing, and on construction in coastal areas. Over 60 percent of our seas lie outside the laws of individual countries, but a UN High Seas Treaty is now helping to protect these international waters.

Fishing and other activities in the high seas are now restricted thanks to a UN High Seas Treaty, which was reached in 2023 after nearly 20 years of negotiations.

What Can I Do?

- Even if you live far from the sea, you can still protect it. Pollution washes down rivers and into the sea, so avoid polluting waterways in your local area. Toxic chemicals and waste materials pollute water and create carbon emissions.

- Think about the products you flush down the toilet or sink at home. Choose eco-friendly cleaning products where possible.

- With a parent or guardian, join a local river or beach clean-up project.

- Think about how you could raise money for a marine charity that protects vulnerable areas.

ENERGY FOR BUILDINGS

With our population growing by about 70 million people a year, we need more buildings than ever before to live and work in. But the materials we use to build and the way we heat and light our homes, schools, and workplaces is putting a huge strain on the planet. We need to modify our buildings and to take steps to reduce energy use inside them.

City fix

About 15 percent of energy-related carbon emissions come from the production of concrete and steel. Heat is also absorbed by the materials we use for our buildings and roads, which can create an "urban heat island" effect – cities can be hotter than their rural surroundings. Wood, if properly sourced and maintained, is a more sustainable building material, which also keeps carbon locked away. We can plant more trees in our cities to cool them too – trees provide useful shade and release water through their leaves.

The city of Melbourne, Australia, has been planting over 3,000 trees each year with the aim of doubling its urban tree cover by 2040.

16

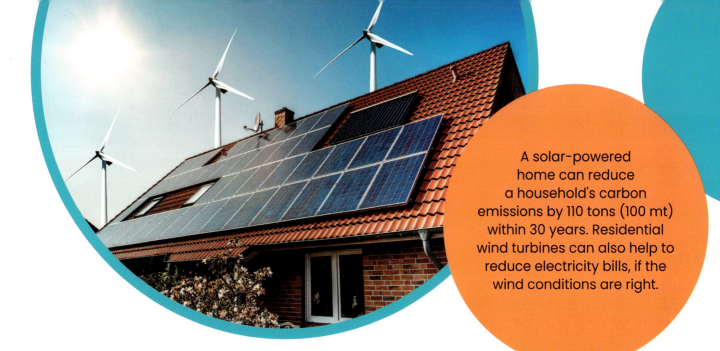

A solar-powered home can reduce a household's carbon emissions by 110 tons (100 mt) within 30 years. Residential wind turbines can also help to reduce electricity bills, if the wind conditions are right.

Hot and cold

Much of the energy we use to heat, cool, and light our buildings comes from fossil fuels. Improved building insulation can reduce energy use for heating and cooling, but we can also wear a sweater instead of heating or use natural ventilation to stay cool. Using energy-efficient light bulbs and appliances (and turning them off when they're not needed) is another way to lower carbon emissions, while changing your energy supplier to one that uses "green" energy, such as wind, water, heat, or solar power, brings even more efficiency.

IT'S A FACT

Iceland is paving the way in green energy – all of Iceland's electricity now comes from renewable sources. About 70 percent is from hydropower and 30 percent from geothermal power stations.

THE FOOD WE EAT

We need to eat a balanced diet to keep healthy, but did you know your diet can also affect the health of the planet? The food choices we make have an impact on the amount of energy that's used and the carbon emissions that are generated. If we all make small, simple changes to our diet, it can add up to make a big difference.

Mealtimes matter

The types of food we eat affect our "carbon footprint" (see page 30). Some fruit and vegetables are grown far away and need to be packaged, stored, and transported, while local, seasonal foods use less energy. Producing meat to be eaten uses even more energy than growing crops. Cattle farming in particular uses a lot of land, cattle feed, and water, and methane is produced when the animals digest. Red meat uses 160 times more land per calorie than potatoes, wheat, and rice, and produces 11 times more carbon emissions.

Eating more plant-based meals, and encouraging your family and friends to as well, is a simple way to reduce your carbon impact.

In this landfill site, methane is being captured and pumped through rubber pipes so it can be stored, rather than released into the atmosphere.

Wasted resources

About a third of all the food we produce for human consumption is lost or wasted. When we throw food away, we're also wasting the precious resources and energy needed to grow, produce, package, and transport it. If food waste ends up in a landfill, it also releases gases such as methane into the atmosphere as it rots. By cutting your food waste, you can reduce your carbon footprint by up to 660 pounds (300 kg) of carbon a year.

What Can I Do?

- Buy local, seasonal food to reduce energy use.

- Try to grow some of your own food, perhaps in a school gardening club or community garden.

- Replace some meat and dairy in your diet with more fruit, vegetables, and pulses.

- Only buy the food you need, and check best-before dates to avoid waste.

- Get creative with leftovers (soup is a good choice!) and compost vegetable peelings.

THE WAY WE TRAVEL

Transportation accounts for nearly a quarter of all global carbon emissions, and this figure is rising more than any other sector, with our growing global population and increasingly connected world. Governments are trying to introduce incentives to change the way we travel and to make it easier for us to reduce the impact we have on our planet.

Global travel

Most of our cars, trucks, trains, ships, and planes run on fossil fuels. Cars are the most common form of transportation, with over 1 billion on our roads. Car use is expected to fall in Europe and the United Stated in future decades, but to rise in Asia. Mile for mile, planes are the most damaging form of transportation, emitting six times more carbon emissions per passenger than a train. We still need to travel, so governments are working to make our transportation more energy efficient.

An electric car emits nearly three times less carbon emissions than a gas or diesel car, even when electricity generation is considered.

GOING ELECTRIC

With its sparsely populated rural regions, Norway hasn't developed a wide public transportation network and cars remain popular. But now the country is leading the way in the shift to electric vehicles. In 2022, four out of five new cars in Norway were fully electric – a change helped by generous financial incentives such as reduced taxes, ferry, and parking fees, a publicly funded network of charging stations, and increased stock to make the cars less expensive. Norway is also working to electrify its city buses, ferries, and domestic flights.

Sustainable transportation

We can all play our part in reducing the fossil fuels we use to get around. Governments are looking to create more safe spaces where people can walk or cycle. For longer distances, you could use public transport or a car-share. Perhaps you could also meet virtually instead of traveling a long distance, minimize flight travel, or consider switching to an electric or hybrid vehicle. Governments are also looking to invest in rail freight, to reduce our reliance on air travel.

Amsterdam in the Netherlands is one of the most bike-friendly cities in the world, with around 320 miles (515 km) of cycle paths and nearly half of all journeys made by bike.

SHOPPING HABITS

The products we buy may look harmless, but they create carbon emissions at each stage of their production, from the raw materials extracted to make them, to the manufacturing processes, packaging, storage, transporting, and shops used to sell them. Whatever product we are buying, we can all be more eco-conscious in our decision-making.

Supply chain

Whether you shop in town or buy online, there are lots of things to think about before you make a purchase. How much energy was used to manufacture the product? Where did the raw materials come from? What waste products were produced? How were the goods transported? How much packaging was used? What lifespan does the product have? How much energy is needed to use it? Can it be recycled or reused in another way?

This is an open copper mine in Spain. Did you know the average smartphone contains gold, silver, and platinum and about 0.5 ounce (15 g) of copper? All these metals need to be mined from the ground.

Shopping around

It's difficult to know the impact of the products we're buying, but ecolabels are now helping to guide consumers. Some ecolabels are required by law – with strict certification guidelines – while others are voluntary, to assess the environmental impact of a product's lifecycle. The Ecolabel Index currently tracks over 450 ecolabels found worldwide. Wherever you can, choose ethical products from companies who use resources responsibly and work to reduce carbon emissions and waste.

Some of the products we buy are given an ecolabel or eco-rating to help us to make informed shopping choices.

 ## What Can I Do?

- Wherever possible, try to choose eco-friendly products.

- Avoid plastic packaging in favor of hemp, bamboo, or recycled material.

- Use reusable shopping bags.

- Buy in bulk to reduce the packaging needed.

- Avoid single-use plastic products and fast fashion – choose items that will last.

- Give customer feedback if you feel a brand could improve its environmental rating.

23

THE POWER OF TECH

While we work to reduce our carbon emissions and to restore and rewild parts of our planet, the challenges we're facing have become a race against time. To restore Earth's natural balance as quickly as possible, scientists are also looking at ways to use technology to help us lessen the impact of climate change.

Carbon capture

Cutting down on carbon emissions is the only way to a sustainable future. But scientists have also found ways to extract and store the carbon we've already created, to speed up the process. Carbon is stored naturally in our forests, soil, and oceans but technology can help us to reach net zero more quickly. It's an expensive process, but filters can be used to capture carbon from factory emissions, as well as extracting carbon from the air with large fans, filters, and chemicals.

Carbon Engineering's first carbon capture plant in Squamish, Canada. Now the company is expanding worldwide to create facilities that can capture a million tons of carbon each year.

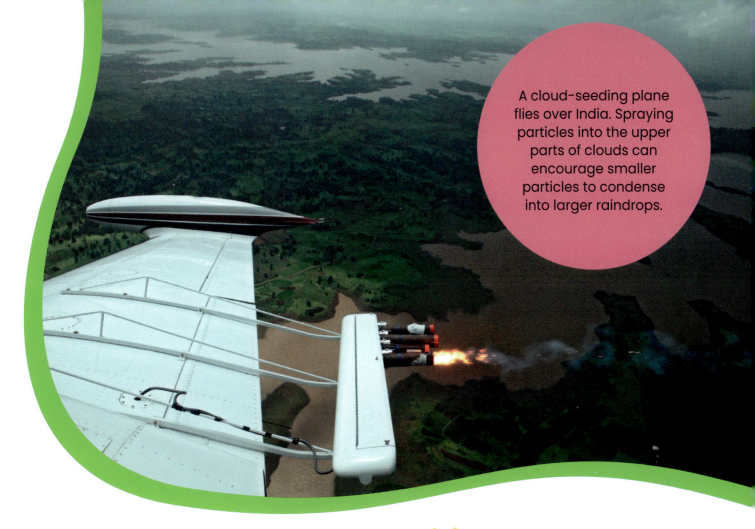

A cloud-seeding plane flies over India. Spraying particles into the upper parts of clouds can encourage smaller particles to condense into larger raindrops.

Geoengineering

Scientists are also looking at ways to help restore conditions in particularly vulnerable areas. Studies have shown that "seeding" clouds can help to increase rainfall in drier regions, and this method could also create more clouds at the poles to reflect the Sun's heat back into space. Scientists have also been considering the use of giant space mirrors to reflect sunlight away from Earth. Geoengineering solutions like these don't get to the root causes of the problem – and need to be checked for safety first – but could help to buy us time while we work to reduce carbon emissions.

ARCTIC REVIVAL

Scientists are looking at different ways to protect ice in the Arctic. One team has suggested using silica (a substance found in sand) to make tiny, reflective beads – thinner than a human hair – that are also hollow, to float on water. Studies on frozen waters in Canada and the United States have shown the beads can make ice 20 percent more reflective to prevent it melting and to help it to grow thicker with age.

REDUCE, REPAIR, REUSE, RECYCLE

One simple measure we can all take to reduce our climate impact is to use less and to reuse or repair the things we already have. Shifting our mindset from "use-and-dispose" to "rethink-and-reuse" is a powerful way to make long-lasting changes. From our shopping and eating habits to the way we travel, we can all make small adjustments to our lifestyle to make a difference.

Make do, and mend

Instead of buying new products, consider looking around for good quality second-hand items. Take the things you don't need to a charity shop so others can use them too. Consider swapping clothes with friends or passing on outgrown items. If something breaks, perhaps it can be easily fixed instead of being replaced? Or perhaps it could be turned into something else? If the demand for new products falls, fewer materials will need to be mined or manufactured to produce them.

In 2021, France introduced a "repairability index" for electronic devices to help consumers see how easy a device is to repair as well as the relative cost and availability of spare parts.

This is a recycled paper printing plant. Recycling paper uses 70 percent less energy than producing paper from raw materials.

Think before you throw

When you make a purchase, think about how long you will use the product or how long it will last. Reuse packaging wherever possible, keep waste to a minimum, and recycle as much as you can. Plastic, for example, is made from oil and it requires a lot of energy to extract, refine, and manufacture. It also doesn't decompose easily, so a lot of plastic waste is burned, which produces carbon emissions.

IT'S A FACT

Recycling a single plastic bottle can save the energy needed to power a light bulb for at least three hours.

MAKING CHANGES

In 2020, Amsterdam became the first city to commit to a circular economy by 2050 – by wasting nothing and recycling everything. The city is focusing on the food residents eat, the products they use, and the city's construction, with an initial goal of halving use of new materials by 2030. During the COVID-19 pandemic and the "cost of living" crisis that followed, the city helped textile businesses cut the cost of clothing repairs to encourage people to fix and reuse the clothes they already have.

SPEAKING OUT

It's easy to think our individual actions won't make a difference to world events, but the way we behave draws attention to governments and businesses, who need the support of voters to be re-elected or paying consumers to survive. By sharing our experiences and conversations with those around us, small changes in behavior can also become social trends that make a real impact.

This is a climate protest in Sydney, Australia. Each generation is bringing new energy to the climate crisis, with a focus on doing well in life by doing good.

Collective action

To tackle climate change we need strong international cooperation between governments and businesses. We need accurate scientific data and the expertise of Indigenous communities in the most vulnerable areas. But the conversations we have with our family and friends and the wider community – about how we travel, what we buy, and where we get our energy from – can also sow the seeds of change. Over time, the messages we give to governments and businesses can force them to act.

Money matters

The climate crisis brings financial considerations, but a 2006 study showed that the benefit of strong early action far outweighs the costs of not acting. Our changing climate has been largely caused by high-income countries. Now they are helping to pay for the damage that poorer, tropical nations are facing. In 2009, high-income countries agreed to raise US$100 billion a year to help less wealthy nations to adapt. In 2022, they agreed to a "loss and damage" fund to help vulnerable nations most impacted by climate change.

What Can I Do?

As well as making simple changes in your own life, you can use your voice to raise awareness of action on climate change:

- Write to your local representative, asking them to meet their net-zero commitments, to help low-income nations with the effects of climate change, and to invest in renewable energy.

- Write to businesses, asking them to reduce carbon emissions in their supply chain and to cut down on packaging.

- With the help of a parent or guardian, you could join a local, national, or international youth campaign that focuses on environmental issues.

To reach net zero, we need to switch to renewable sources of energy, such as wind farms, as soon as possible. There are cost implications but transforming to a green economy can also unlock new opportunities and jobs.

IT'S A FACT

The World Bank has predicted that every US$1 of investment towards a green economy brings an average of US$4 in benefits.

GLOSSARY

atmosphere The layers of gases that surround a planet.

carbon emissions Gases – primarily carbon dioxide – that are produced when fossil fuels are burned, or through other human activities.

carbon footprint The amount of greenhouse gases, such as carbon dioxide and methane, released into the atmosphere as a result of our actions.

circular economy An economic system that keeps materials, products, and services in circulation for as long as possible in a sustainable, environmentally friendly way.

climate The long-term weather conditions in a particular place.

COVID-19 An infectious disease that emerged in 2019 and spread around the world as a pandemic.

deforestation Clearing trees from a forest so the land can be used for other purposes.

drought A long period of abnormally low rainfall, leading to water shortages.

freight Goods transported in bulk, by truck, train, ship, or aircraft.

geoengineering A way of intervening in the natural processes that affect Earth's climate, to reduce the impact of climate change.

geothermal Heat energy found within Earth's crust.

glacier A large body of slow-moving ice that has formed on land.

green economy An economic system guided by environmental principles.

greenhouse gases Gases in Earth's atmosphere, such as carbon dioxide and methane, that trap the Sun's heat, warming our planet.

hydropower A type of power station that uses the energy from flowing water to generate electricity.

indigenous The original, earliest known inhabitants of a region, or their descendants.

Industrial Revolution A transition to new manufacturing processes that began in the 18th century in Europe and the US.

mindset A habitual way of thinking.

polar regions The areas around the North and South Poles.

renewable energy Energy that comes from a source, such as the wind or the Sun, that can't be used up.

resilient Able to withstand difficult conditions.

rewild Restore land to its natural state.

supply chain The processes involved in the production and distribution of goods.

sustainable A way of doing things that can continue for a long time, without using up natural resources or causing damage.

United Nations An international organization founded in 1945. Its 193 member states work together to maintain international peace, security, and cooperation.

World Bank An international organization, with 189 member countries, that provides loans and grants to the governments of low- and middle-income nations to improve their economies.

World Economic Forum An international organization that brings together individuals and political and business leaders each year to discuss issues that affect the global economy.

FURTHER INFORMATION

Books

Climate Change by Don Nardo, ReferencePoint Press, 2024

Climate Change by William D. Adams, World Book, 2024

What Is Climate Change? by Louise Spilsbury, Wayland, 2021

Websites

www.un.org/sustainabledevelopment/student-resources
This is a selection of resources to help you create a more sustainable world.

www.un.org/actnow
Find out how you can join the UN campaign for individual action on climate change.

www.climatekids.nasa.gov
Check out fun activities and resources to learn more about our climate.

INDEX

adapting 5, 8, 9, 12, 15, 29
agriculture 5, 10, 11, 18
Amazon Rainforest 10–11
animals 8, 9, 10, 12, 18
Arctic 12–13, 25
Arctic Council 13
Australia 16, 28

Brazil 10
buildings 4, 5, 8, 9, 10, 16, 17
businesses 7, 11, 27, 28, 29

Canada 13, 24, 25
carbon capture 24
carbon dioxide 4, 5, 6, 10, 14
carbon emissions 4, 5, 6, 7, 9, 11, 14, 15, 16, 17, 18, 20, 22, 23, 24, 27, 29
carbon footprint 18, 19
China 11
cities 7, 11, 16, 21, 27
climate-resistant crops 9
clothing 7, 23, 26, 27
coastal erosion 9, 14
Colombia 11
conservation projects 9, 13, 14, 15
construction industry 5, 9, 10, 15, 16, 27
coral reefs 9, 14, 15

deforestation 5, 10
drought 8, 9, 10

energy 7, 16–17, 18, 19, 20, 22, 27, 28, 29
  renewable 7, 17, 29

factories 4, 7, 24
farming 5, 10, 18
financial cost 21, 29
flooding 4, 8, 9, 14
food 5, 8, 9, 10, 11, 12, 18–19, 26, 27
forests 5, 9, 10, 11, 24
fossil fuels 4, 13, 17, 20, 21, 27
France 26

geoengineering 25
Global Ocean Alliance 15
governments 6, 7, 20, 21, 28, 29
greenhouse gases 4, 5, 6, 10, 12, 14, 18, 19

Honduras 9

Iceland 13, 17
India 9, 10, 25
Indigenous communities 13, 28
Indonesia 14
Industrial Revolution 4, 6

manufacturing 22, 26, 27
Mauna Loa Observatory 5
methane 4, 12, 18, 19
mining 5, 10, 22, 26, 27

net zero 7, 24, 29
Netherlands 21, 27
Norway 13, 21

oceans 4, 8, 12, 14–15, 24

packaging 18, 22, 23, 27, 29
Pakistan 11

Paris Agreement 6
plants 5, 8, 12, 18
plastic 23, 27
polar regions 12–13, 25
pollution 8, 15
population growth 5, 16, 20

rainfall 8, 9, 10, 12, 25
recycling 11, 22, 23, 26–27
restoration projects 9, 11, 13, 15, 24, 25

sea levels 4, 12, 14
shopping 7, 22–23, 26, 27, 28
solar power 7, 17
Spain 22
supply chain 7, 22, 29

technology 24–25
temperature 4, 5, 6, 7, 8, 9, 10, 12, 14, 15
transportation 4, 18, 19, 20–21, 22, 26, 28
trees 5, 9, 10, 11, 16
trillion trees initiative 11

UN Climate Change Conference 6, 7, 10
UN High Seas Treaty 15
United Nations 6, 7, 10, 15

waste 19, 22, 23, 27
weather 4, 8–9, 10, 12, 13, 14, 25
wind power 7, 17, 29
World Bank 29
World Economic Forum 11